Scientists

Carlotta Hacker

Crabtree Publishing Company

Dedication

This series is dedicated to every woman who has followed her dreams and to every young girl who hopes to do the same. While overcoming great odds and often oppression, the remarkable women in this series have triumphed in their fields. Their dedication, hard work, and excellence can serve as an inspiration to all—young and old, male and female. Women in Profile is both an acknowledgment of and a tribute to these great women.

Project Manager
Lauri Seidlitz
Crabtree Editor
Virginia Mainprize
Copy Editors
Leslie Strudwick
Krista McLuskey
Design and Layout
Warren Clark

Published by Crabtree Publishing Company

350 Fifth Avenue, Suite 3308
New York, NY
USA 10018

360 York Road, R.R. 4
Niagara-on-the-Lake
Ontario, Canada
L0S 1J0

Copyright © 1998 WEIGL EDUCATIONAL PUBLISHERS LIMITED. All rights reserved. No part of this publication may be reproduced, stored in a retrieval system or transmitted in any form or by any means, electronic, mechanical, photocopying, recording, or otherwise, without the prior written permission of Weigl Educational Publishers Limited.

Cataloging-in-Publication Data

Hacker, Carlotta.
      Scientists / Carlotta Hacker.
            p. cm. — (Women in profile)
      Includes bibliographical references and index.
      Summary: Chronicles the lives and achievements of noted female scientists, including astronomer Jocelyn Bell Burnell, primatologist Dian Fossey, and anthropologist Margaret Mead.
      ISBN 0-7787-0006-2 (RLB). — ISBN 0-7787-0028-3 (PB)
      1. Women scientists—Biography—Juvenile literature. 2. Women in science—History—20th century—Juvenile literature. [1. Women scientists. 2. Scientists. 3. Women—Biography.] I. Title. II. Series.
Q141.H2163 1998   98-10659
509.2'2—dc21   CIP
[B]   AC

Photograph Credits
Every reasonable effort has been made to trace ownership and to obtain permission to reprint copyright material. The publishers would be pleased to have any errors or omissions brought to their attention so that they may be corrected in subsequent printings.
Archive Photos: pages 7, 16, 39; Jocelyn Bell Burnell: page 10; Columbia University: page 41; Corbis-Bettmann: page 42; Dian Fossey Gorilla Fund International: pages 19, 23; Globe Photos, Inc.: page 17; Photofest: pages 12, 31, 35, 44; Open University: pages 6, 9, 11; Science Photo Library: cover, pages 24, 28, 29 (John Reader), 37; Tom Stack & Associates: pages 20, 21; Topham Picture Point: page 18; UPI/Corbis-Bettmann: pages 13, 15, 25, 27, 30, 33, 34, 36, 38, 40, 43, 45; U.S. Fish and Wildlife Service: page 14 (Rex Gary Schmidt); Vasser College Libraries: page 8.

Contents

More Women in Profile

Scientists

More than 1,600 years ago there was a woman scientist called Hypatia. She lived in Egypt, and she was a mathematician. In those days, it was not thought odd for a woman to study the sciences, but this outlook changed over the years.

By the nineteenth century, there were hardly any women scientists. They could not get the proper training. Some girls might be allowed to learn math, but they were not taught chemistry or biology. Such subjects were considered far too difficult for the female mind.

Despite this attitude, a few women did manage to get educated in the sciences. They then met another block: no university would accept them. Only during the past fifty years have women been able to study the sciences on much the same terms as men.

Since then, many women have led the way in **physics**, biology, **astronomy**, mathematics, and chemistry—almost every branch of science. Several have made such important discoveries that they have been awarded the Nobel Prize.

Today, there are thousands of women scientists. The six featured here are all world famous, though they are not necessarily the six most famous. They have been chosen because they show some of the fields in which women scientists have excelled. Several more scientists are mentioned at the end of the book. Nobel Prize-winning scientists are featured in a separate volume in this series, one that focuses on women who have been awarded the Nobel Prize.

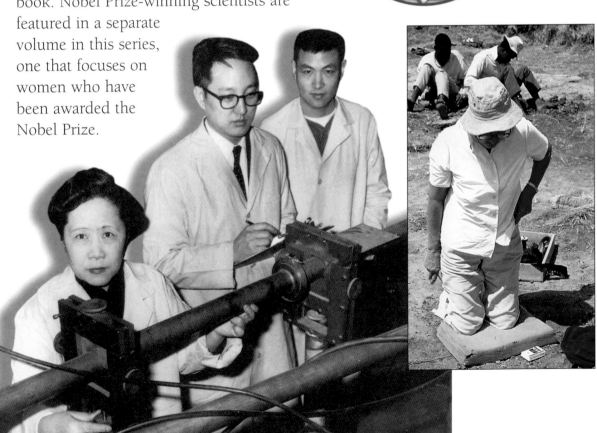

"Radio astronomers are aware that they would probably be the first people to come into contact with other civilizations."

Jocelyn Bell Burnell

Irish Astronomer

Early Years

Jocelyn was born in Northern Ireland where her parents had a large country house called Solitude. The house had belonged to the family for two hundred years. There were no neighbors close by, but Jocelyn played with her two sisters and her brother. They made up their own games and explored the countryside together.

Jocelyn began her education at a small school in a nearby town. The teaching was not good, and she failed an important exam called the eleven-plus when she was eleven years old. This was a terrible blow. The eleven-plus decided a student's future. Students who passed went to a high school that prepared them for university. Those who failed were given a less academic education.

Fortunately for Jocelyn, her parents could afford to send her to a private school. They enrolled her at a Quaker school in England. Jocelyn loved it. "Going to boarding school gave me a new start," she said later. She made lots of new friends and was captain of the field hockey team. She also did well at her studies. At the age of eighteen, she was accepted by the University of Glasgow in Scotland.

BACKGROUNDER

Quakers

Jocelyn's family belong to a Christian group known as the Quakers. Quakers are very peace loving and will not fight in wars. They are called Quakers because their founder, George Fox, told his followers to "tremble at the name of the Lord." The official name of the group is the Religious Society of Friends.

George Fox founded the Quakers in 1646.

Developing Skills

Jocelyn went to university with the hope of becoming an astronomer. She had been interested in **astronomy** since the age of thirteen when she had visited the Armagh Observatory with her father. Jocelyn's father was an architect, and he had been asked to design an addition to the observatory.

The staff at the observatory let Jocelyn look through their huge telescope. She was amazed at what she saw. She had never dreamed there were so many stars in the sky. The astronomers told her that it was possible to study the skies in the daytime by using **radio waves**. Jocelyn decided to make radio astronomy her career.

This was easier said than done, for there was fierce competition for jobs in astronomy. Jocelyn decided to major in **physics**, but even that was difficult. After her first year at university, she was the only woman in a class of three hundred men. She had to put up with a lot of teasing.

After getting her bachelor's degree, Jocelyn went to Cambridge University in England to study astronomy. The university had started to build a huge radio telescope, and Jocelyn became a member of the team that was building it.

Women have been astronomers since the nineteenth century. Maria Mitchell (far left) was an American astronomer who studied sunspots and satellites. In 1848, she became the first woman to become a member of the American Academy of Arts and Sciences.

For two years, Jocelyn and a handful of other students built this unusual telescope. They hammered one thousand posts into the ground, each of which was 9 feet (3 meters) high.

Between the posts, they hung two thousand antennae. There were also two hundred **transformers**. The whole thing was strung together with 120 miles (200 kilometers) of wire. When completed, the radio telescope covered an area the size of fifty-seven tennis courts. It was ready for use in July 1967.

Jocelyn had the job of studying the **data** gathered by the telescope. This was an enormous task. Four radio beams scanned the sky, and their signals were recorded on chart paper. One scan of a part of the sky produced 400 feet (122 meters) of paper.

The data came in far more quickly than Jocelyn could study it. By November, her backlog of paper measured a third of a mile (over 0.5 kilometers). Yet she would not cut corners. She studied each mark on the paper carefully. It was because she was so careful that she made one of the greatest discoveries in modern astronomy.

BACKGROUNDER

Radio Astronomy

Astronomy is almost as old as humankind. Originally, all astronomy was done by sight, either by the naked eye or by looking through a telescope. Since the 1930s, it has also been possible to "look" at the sky by means of radio waves. Objects in space give off radio waves, and these can be collected and measured by a radio telescope. Radio telescopes can locate stars and other objects that cannot be seen by a normal telescope.

Jocelyn's analysis of her data was complicated. She had to learn to tell the difference between radio waves from stars and signals from radio and television broadcasts.

"Though slight in stature, she could swing a twenty-pound sledge hammer by the time she left Cambridge."
Nicholas Wade in *Science* magazine

Quick Notes

- Radio telescopes also pick up signals from airplanes, refrigerator motors, and passing cars. These signals can interfere with those from space.

- Jocelyn remains an active Quaker. From 1978 to 1990, she represented the Quakers as a member of both the British Council of Churches and the Scottish Council of Churches.

- Each year, Jocelyn helps plan the Edinburgh International Science Festival.

"I began to remember that I had seen this particular bit of scruff before, and from the same part of the sky."

Accomplishments

One day in October 1967, Jocelyn noticed some small ink marks that looked different from everything else on the chart paper. This "bit of scruff" covered less than half an inch (1.75 centimeters) and could easily have been overlooked.

Jocelyn remembered that she had seen something like this before in the same part of the sky. When she checked, she found that the signals came at regular intervals. Could they be signals from creatures in a distant solar system? Her supervisor thought it possible. Soon, they were all making jokes about "little green men."

Some months later, Jocelyn found similar signals from another part of the sky. "That removed the worry about little green men," she said later. "There wouldn't be two lots signalling us." After more research, she decided that the signals were caused by rotating stars that gave off radio signals in a narrow beam. Each time the star spun around, its signal was picked up by the radio telescope.

By January 1968, Jocelyn had found two more of these objects. They are now known as pulsars, or pulsating radio stars. They are very dense, burned-out stars. More than six hundred have been located since Jocelyn identified them. The discovery caused great excitement. Jocelyn's supervisor, Antony Hewish, was awarded a Nobel Prize in physics for the discovery, since he was the leader of the team.

Jocelyn was only twenty-four when she made her world-famous discovery. Since then, she has taught at several universities. She could not stay in the same job for more than a few years because her husband, Martin Burnell, worked for the government and was moved about England. Jocelyn went with him. Only after they separated could Jocelyn choose where she would live and work.

Since 1991, Jocelyn has been professor of physics at the Open University, north of London. The university provides home-study courses for adults anywhere in Britain. Each year, more than a thousand students take Jocelyn's astronomy course. Meanwhile, she continues to do research. Much of her research has been on X-ray astronomy. One of Jocelyn's recent projects was finding out more about pulsars.

BACKGROUNDER

The Nobel Prize

Fred Hoyle, a leading British astronomer, was furious that Jocelyn had not been awarded the Nobel Prize. He said that her professors at Cambridge had stolen the discovery from her. Jocelyn had done much more than "search and search through a great mass of records," he said. Not only had she found the signals, but she had also noticed that they changed position with the stars. Her discovery came because she did not accept what many people believed was impossible. Jocelyn did not share Fred Hoyle's outrage. She told a journalist, "I believe it would demean the Nobel Prizes if they were awarded to research students, except in very exceptional cases, and I do not believe this is one of them."

One of Jocelyn's most exciting jobs was manager of the James Clerk Maxwell Telescope project. The telescope is on top of a mountain in Hawaii and is owned by Canada, Great Britain, and the Netherlands.

"Most people don't know where to look for the most fascinating things at the beach. All they can see is a few shells and the occasional crab. But there are all kinds of things going on right under the surface of the sand."

Rachel Carson

American Marine Biologist and Science Writer

Early Years

When Rachel was a child, she loved to sit under a tree with one of her cats on her knee. Listening to its soft purr, she would become aware of other sounds around her—leaves rustling and birds twittering. If she listened very carefully, she could even hear her parents' horses chomping the grass.

Rachel lived on a farm in Springdale, Pennsylvania. Her parents, Robert and Maria, had taught her to enjoy the sights and sounds of the countryside. Even as a small child, Rachel could recognize a bird by its song. She could name the different fish in the stream.

Rachel was the youngest of three children. Like the others, she was encouraged to use her imagination. She wrote her first poem when she was eight. When she was ten, she wrote a story called "A Battle in the Clouds." It was published in a magazine.

BACKGROUNDER

Marine Biology

Marine biologists study everything that lives and grows in the sea. This includes plants, corals, fish, jellyfish, and many other creatures. Marine biologists also study how the living things of the sea are affected by their surroundings. When part of the sea is polluted, some **species** may get sick and die.

Rachel's love of nature began on her family farm.

Developing Skills

Rachel did well at school and won a scholarship to the Pennsylvania College for Women. She meant to major in English because she wanted to be a writer, but she soon changed her mind. After taking a biology course in her junior year, she realized how much she enjoyed learning about plants and animals. She decided to major in **zoology**.

Rachel got her bachelor's degree in 1929. She spent the next summer at the Marine Biology Laboratory in Woods Hole, Massachusetts. There she saw the ocean for the first time. It opened a whole new world to her. She saw **sea anemones**, **sea urchins**, and many other creatures that lived in the ocean. She decided to work in marine biology.

In 1936, Rachel joined the United States Bureau of Fisheries. The bureau did not usually hire women, but Rachel had top marks in the entrance exam. She was the second woman scientist ever to work at the bureau. She produced the **bulletins** that the bureau published. Rachel's work was so outstanding that she was eventually made editor-in-chief.

Rachel spent hours studying the rich life of the sea and shorelines.

Rachel wrote for the bulletins as well as edited them. She also wrote for magazines. Her first success was the article "Undersea" which was published by the *Atlantic Monthly* magazine. Rachel later enlarged this article into a book called *Under the Sea-Wind*. It described the sea and shore in North Carolina.

This first book did not sell many copies. Nor did Rachel's next book which was about protected wildlife areas. It was her third book that made her famous. Published in 1951, it was called *The Sea around Us*. Rachel had taken years researching the book that told the story of the sea from earliest times. It described everything from the smallest sea creatures to the great underwater mountains in the deepest oceans.

No one had ever told the story of the sea like this. The book was very popular. It won the National Book Award and several other honors. So many copies were sold that Rachel was able to retire from her job with the United States Fish and Wildlife Service. She became a full-time writer.

BACKGROUNDER

The United States Fish and Wildlife Service

In 1940, the Bureau of Fisheries was merged with the Bureau of Biological Survey to form the Fish and Wildlife Service. Its main aim was "to conserve the nation's wild birds, mammals, fishes, and other forms of wildlife." Its job was to see that wildlife survived and did not suffer harm. The bureau also published bulletins and leaflets about American wildlife.

Before sitting down to write, Rachel did extensive research. She went undersea diving during the summer of 1949 to help prepare for **The Sea around Us.**

BACKGROUNDER

Pesticides

A pesticide is a liquid, a powder, or a gas that kills pests. Insecticides (which kill insects), herbicides (which kill weeds), and fungicides (which kill **fungi**) are all pesticides. Some pesticides do not harm the environment, but others should be used with great care. During the late 1940s and 1950s, a chemical called DDT was a widely used pesticide. Farmers thought it was a wonderful invention. They could look forward to a good harvest if they sprayed their crops with DDT. In tropical countries, DDT was often used because it killed the mosquitoes that spread **malaria**. Until *Silent Spring* was published, people did not know that DDT polluted the soil and could kill animals. Today, DDT is banned in Canada, the United States, and many other countries. Less dangerous pesticides are used to control insects. However, some chemical companies still make DDT. They sell it to less-developed countries that have difficulty growing enough food to feed their people.

Accomplishments

Rachel's most important book was about the use of pesticides. She had received a letter from a woman who said that spraying pesticides had killed all the birds in her bird sanctuary. In the 1950s, most American farmers sprayed their crops with a pesticide called DDT. It was the latest way of killing grubs and insects. Rachel believed that DDT was killing other things as well. It was especially dangerous when sprayed from the air, for it could drift beyond the farmers' fields.

If DDT could kill birds, could it also harm humans? If people ate crops that had been sprayed, could they be poisoned slowly? Rachel decided to find out.

Rachel spent four years researching the subject. She wrote to experts in chemistry and other branches of science, asking for information. By the time she had gathered all the **data**, she had decided that DDT should be banned. It was far too dangerous to be used on crops.

"I can remember no time when I wasn't interested in the out-of-doors and the whole world of nature."

Rachel's book *Silent Spring* showed how DDT could poison the whole environment. After DDT was sprayed on crops, it found its way into the soil. The rains washed the pesticide into the rivers where it killed the fish. It then killed the birds that ate the fish. At each stage, it harmed something.

Shortly before the book was published, a section from it was printed in the *New Yorker* magazine. The chemical companies that made DDT were furious when they read the article. They tried to prevent Rachel's book from being published. They would lose a lot of money if farmers stopped using pesticides.

The **controversy** continued after the book came out. Some people sided with Rachel. Others sided with the chemical companies. Either way, Rachel had achieved her goal. She had made people think about DDT and discuss its effects. Rachel did not live long enough to see DDT banned in the United States. She died only two years after *Silent Spring* was published, knowing she had started something big.

Rachel had alerted the world to the danger of misusing pesticides. As well, she had shown that nature needs protecting. Many of the ideas we have today about protecting the environment can be traced back to Rachel's book.

In 1963, a special television show called "The Silent Spring of Rachel Carson" featured a debate between Rachel and people from chemical manufacturing companies.

Quick Notes

- Rachel's book *The Edge of the Sea* was made into a movie that won an Academy Award.

- Rachel raised her nieces after their mother died.

- When one of Rachel's nieces died as an adult, Rachel adopted her son.

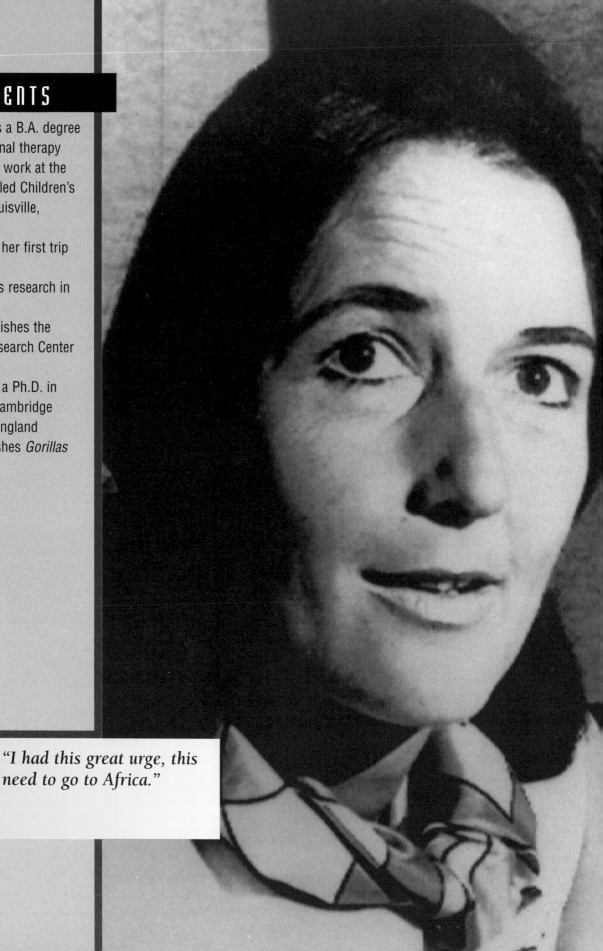

"I had this great urge, this need to go to Africa."

Dian Fossey

American Primatologist

Early Years

During her childhood in San Francisco, California, Dian longed to have a dog or cat as a pet. She was not allowed. Her parents had divorced when she was six, and her stepfather was very strict. He let Dian keep a goldfish, but nothing else. She was very unhappy when it died.

Dian loved animals, and she wanted to work with them when she grew up. After high school, she began to train as a veterinarian, an animal doctor. She failed her second year, and she switched to occupational therapy. After finishing her training, Dian became director of occupational therapy at a children's hospital in Louisville, Kentucky. She loved the job, but her thoughts were often far away in Africa. She had read about the mountain gorillas of Central Africa, and she wanted to go and see them.

BACKGROUNDER

Occupational Therapy

Occupational therapists help people learn the skills they need to function in everyday life. Sometimes the people they help are sick or have a disability. Describing the children at the hospital, Dian wrote: "These children have a variety of physical and emotional disabilities…. They need a tremendous amount of care and kindness to make them feel life is worth living."

Dian's childhood love for animals later became her passion for saving the mountain gorilla from extinction.

Developing Skills

BACKGROUNDER

Mountain Gorillas

The mountain gorillas are the largest of all the apes. A fully grown male can weigh 400 pounds (182 kilograms) and stand 6 feet (2 meters) tall. They were first recognized as a separate **species** in 1902. All the mountain gorillas in the world live in one small area of Central Africa. This area is covered with thick rain forest and is high in the mountains. It is part of three different countries: Rwanda, Uganda, and the Democratic Republic of the Congo.

In 1963, Dian borrowed $8,000 from her bank and took a seven-week holiday in Africa. At last, she was going to see the mountain gorillas of the Congo!

On the way, she stopped in Tanzania to meet Mary and Louis Leakey who were working there. Dian wanted to meet the Leakeys because they had helped the English researcher Jane Goodall begin a study of chimpanzees. The Leakeys believed that by studying the great apes, people could learn more about humans. They were pleased that Dian was interested in the gorillas. While Dian was with the Leakeys, she fell and hurt her ankle. It seemed she would have to cancel her trip to see the gorillas.

Dian did not do so. Two weeks later, she was hobbling up a mountain in the Congo. She heard the gorillas before she saw them. They were letting out high-pitched screams, and a huge male gorilla was making a loud "pok pok" sound as he drummed his chest with his fists. Dian was thrilled. She decided to come back and study these animals.

Dian's work has helped people better understand mountain gorillas and want to save them.

Dian had to wait three years to return to Africa. In 1966, Louis Leakey visited Louisville on a lecture tour. He met Dian again and was impressed by her eagerness. By the time he left, he had agreed to hire her to do a study of the mountain gorillas.

Dian arrived in Africa later that year. She set up camp at Kabara, in Virungas National Park in the Congo. Several groups of gorillas lived there, but Dian could not get near them. They ran away whenever they saw her.

To make the gorillas less nervous, Dian pretended to be a gorilla. She copied the sounds they made when they were happy. She pretended to eat their favorite food. She even learned to walk the way they did, using her knuckles as well as her feet.

"I scratched my scalp noisily to make a sound familiar to gorillas, who do a great deal of scratching."

Little by little, the gorillas became used to Dian. They let her get close to them and follow them through the jungle.

Accomplishments

After only six months, Dian was forced to leave the Congo because civil war had broken out. She moved across the border to Rwanda, where she set up camp in the Volcanoes National Park. She called her camp the Karisoke Research Center.

Four groups of gorillas lived near the camp, but they were even more nervous than the gorillas in the Congo. This was because they had been hunted. **Poachers** killed the animals for their skins or captured them to sell to zoos. Dian could not get near the gorillas.

Again, she pretended to be a gorilla. At first, the gorillas kept their distance, but slowly they accepted her. It was a great day when one of them stretched out a hand and touched her fingers.

For the next thirteen years, Dian lived and worked among the mountain gorillas. She discovered that they were gentle, intelligent animals. They could make fifteen sounds, each meaning something different. They lived in family groups and would fight to the death to protect a member of their family.

NIGERIA

CENTRAL AFRICAN REPUBLIC

CAMEROON

EQUATORIAL GUINEA

CONGO

UGANDA

KENYA

GABON

DEMOCRATIC REPUBLIC OF THE CONGO

RWANDA
BURUNDI

Atlantic Ocean

TANZANIA

Location of the World's Gorillas

- Mountain gorilla (Volcanoes National Park)
- Eastern lowland gorilla
- Western lowland gorilla

The poachers continued their work, and there were several deaths over the years. One day, they killed a gorilla called Digit who was one of Dian's favorites. She was so upset and angry that she reported it to newspapers all over the world. This caused such a stir that the Digit Fund was set up to protect the gorillas. Many people still give money to the fund.

The fund paid for guards to patrol the national park, but the guards could not keep out all the poachers. A few months later, Dian found two more dead gorillas. Dian's long battle against the poachers began to affect her health, and she went home to the United States in 1980. She lived there for three years, teaching at Cornell University and writing her book, *Gorillas in the Mist*.

Dian returned to Karisoke in 1983, prepared to spend another long period studying the gorillas. Two years later, she was dead. She had been murdered in her bedroom during the night.

The murderer was never caught. Many people think that Dian was killed by poachers.

Quick Notes

- The movie *Gorillas in the Mist* (1988) is about Dian's life and work among the gorillas.

- In 1970, Dian enrolled at Cambridge University in England to study for a degree in zoology.

"I am more comfortable with gorillas than with people."

Dian did everything she could to stop the poachers. She often burned the traps used to catch gorillas and other animals.

"*I am lucky enough to have been involved with work that belongs to everyone, since it concerns the human origins that are common to the whole human race.*"

Mary Leakey

English Paleontologist and Archeologist

Early Days

Mary was eleven when she first became interested in archeology. "It was like a treasure hunt," she said, "searching through the earth at a site in France." There she found tools, flint blades, and many other things—all of them thousands of years old.

Mary had been born in England, but her family often went to France. Her father was an artist, and he liked to paint the European countryside. One year, they visited some ancient cave paintings. The paintings had been made more than ten thousand years ago. By then, Mary knew she wanted to study archeology.

Mary loved visiting archeological sites. She thought it was like being on a treasure hunt.

BACKGROUNDER

Paleontology and Archeology

Paleontology is the study of fossils. Fossils are the remains or traces of animals or plants that lived long ago. They are found in rock. By studying fossils, scientists can discover what plants and animals looked like millions of years ago. They can date the plants and animals according to the age of the rock in which their fossils are found. By dating fossils, much can be discovered about what the world was like in **prehistoric** times. Archeology is also a study of past times, but it concentrates on more recent eras than paleontology. Archeologists dig up ancient cities and campsites to learn about past cultures. They study the tools, weapons, pottery, and other things they find.

Developing Skills

W hen she was seventeen, Mary became an assistant to the archeologist Dorothy Liddell. For the next three summers, she worked at a site in England and made drawings of the stone tools that were found there. During the winters, she attended lectures at the University of London.

Mary's drawings of the tools were published in several scientific journals. They attracted a lot of attention and led to her meeting Louis Leakey. Louis was researching the origins of humans. He was so impressed by Mary's drawings that he asked her to do the illustrations for his book *Adam's Ancestors*.

This was the beginning of a lifelong partnership. Mary and Louis were married in 1936, and they worked together until Louis's death in 1972.

Much of their work was done at the Olduvai Gorge in Tanzania. Louis had found some ancient stone tools there, and he was convinced that the earliest humans had lived in that part of Africa. The first time Mary and Louis went there together, they found some fragments from an ancient human skull.

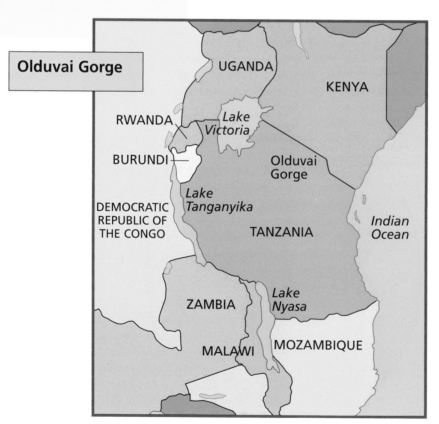

In 1937, Mary and Louis **excavated** sites in Kenya where they discovered some human bones that were between three and ten thousand years old. While Louis was helping the British during World War II, Mary continued excavating. She found thousands of stone tools. Some of them were the oldest that had been found anywhere in the world.

Mary made an even more exciting discovery in 1948. She was digging on an island in Lake Victoria, when she came across the fossil of an ape's skull, at least twenty-five million years old. Mary and Louis named the ape *Proconsul africanus.*

Mary and her husband, Louis, made some of the world's most important archeological discoveries.

"I saw some interesting-looking bone fragments lying on the sloping surface, and letting my eyes travel upwards, I saw a tooth.... Not only was it a Proconsul tooth, but it was in place in a jaw."

Accomplishments

Like others who worked in the field, Mary and Louis hoped to find "the missing link"—the ape-like creature that would prove that apes and humans have a common ancestor. The Leakeys thought that *Proconsul africanus* might be the long-sought link. This idea made them even more eager to do further excavations. They decided that the best place to begin would be the Olduvai Gorge in Tanzania.

In 1951, Mary and Louis set up their tents beside the Olduvai Gorge and began to excavate the area. Mary made her big find eight years later. That day, she was working at the site alone because Louis had a fever. Brushing aside some soil, she saw a fossil of some teeth. In great excitement, she rushed back to camp to tell Louis.

During the next few days, they carefully removed the earth around the fossil. It turned out to be a skull that looked as if it had belonged to a human. Because of the rock in which it was found, they knew that it must be 1.75 million years old. They called it *Zinjanthropus*. Although it was more ape than human, it was still an important discovery.

"This was a wildly exciting find that would delight human paleontologists all over the world."

Zinjanthropus brought the Leakeys fame throughout the world, and people were eager to fund their work. Mary and Louis could now hire a team of helpers to work full time. This soon brought results. During the next few years, they found several more important fossils, as well as the tools of an early human. These findings proved that humans had been living in Africa for more than two million years.

During the late 1960s, Louis suffered from poor health, so Mary took over as leader of the team. She continued in this role after her husband's death.

In 1978, Mary made an important discovery. In the Serengeti Plain south of the Olduvai Gorge, she found fossilized footprints in a stretch of volcanic rock. They looked just like human footprints, and they were 3.5 million years old.

Mary lost the sight of one eye a few years later, and she had to cut back on her research. She wrote a book about her life. *Disclosing the Past* was published in 1984.

Mary stayed in Africa for the rest of her life, spending her last years in Kenya. She had become one of the most important paleontologists of the twentieth century.

Quick Notes

- *Zinjanthropus* means "East African man." The Leakeys nicknamed their find "Dear Boy."

- Mary received numerous awards, including the gold medal of the Society of Women Geographers.

- In addition to their other finds, the Leakeys discovered some ancient rock paintings in Africa.

Archeological digs require enormous patience. Archeologists must handle artifacts carefully because most are extremely fragile.

"Life in the twentieth century is like a parachute jump—you have to get it right the first time."

Margaret Mead

American Anthropologist

Early Years

Margaret was born in Philadelphia, Pennsylvania, where her father was a university professor. Her mother was a sociologist, studying how people behave and live. The family hoped that Margaret, too, would become a sociologist. When Margaret was only eight, her grandmother taught her to observe younger children and take notes on what they did. This was Margaret's earliest training in sociology.

Margaret was proud of her unusual family. Her parents had ideas that were ahead of their time. They thought that a woman should have a career if she wanted. They also believed that women should be allowed to vote in elections. Margaret's mother was a **suffragette** who worked to get women the vote.

BACKGROUNDER

Women in the Early 1900s

In the early 1900s, most women from wealthy families did not go out to work. They were expected to marry, stay home, and have children. However, a few chose a different way of life. They studied at universities and became teachers, scientists, lawyers, doctors, and other professionals.

As a young girl, Margaret wanted to be a painter.

Developing Skills

Like her sisters, Margaret was given a good education. She attended high school in Pennsylvania and then went on to college. By the time she was twenty-two, she had a master's degree from Columbia University.

Despite her early training, Margaret did not become a sociologist. At Columbia, she took a course given by the famous anthropologist, Franz Boas. Professor Boas was worried that, in the modern age, many of the world's cultures were disappearing. People were forgetting their traditions.

Listening to Professor Boas, Margaret realized what she wanted to do with her life. She would study these vanishing cultures before they were gone. "Anthropology has to be done now," she said. "Other things can wait."

Margaret's first field trip was to Samoa, a group of islands in the Pacific. She chose Samoa because it had not been touched by the modern world. Few outsiders had visited the islands. She arrived in 1925 and spent the next nine months studying the Samoan people's customs and traditions.

Places Margaret Mead Visited

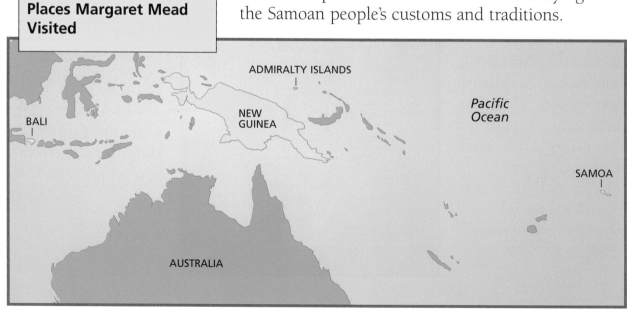

Margaret lived with the villagers so that she could get to know how they thought and behaved. She found the teenage girls especially interesting. They seemed much happier than American teenagers and seldom quarreled with their parents. Margaret was so impressed that she wrote a book about them called *Coming of Age in Samoa*. It quickly became a bestseller.

During the next few years, Margaret made several other field trips and wrote about what she found. On one trip, she went to the Admiralty Islands off the coast of New Guinea. On another, she went to Bali in Indonesia. She always learned the language so that she could talk with the people and live among them. This way, she became part of the community, rather than being an outsider looking in.

Margaret had another great advantage. She wrote well. She could describe her studies in a way ordinary people could understand. By the time World War II broke out in 1939, she had written several books and was well known both at home and abroad.

Margaret spent two years in New Guinea studying the customs of the headhunters. When she returned, she brought back several of their trophy heads.

"I am glad that I am living at this ... very crucial period in human history."

Accomplishments

After the war, Margaret began to study the American family. She saw that Americans were facing changes that affected their family life. Fewer people lived in the country. Many had moved to the cities to find jobs.

When a family lived in a small country community, it was a close-knit group. Grandparents, aunts, uncles, and cousins lived nearby and helped their family. They joined together to celebrate special occasions. All this was lost when people moved to a city. There, they often felt lonely and helpless.

Margaret was especially interested in the problems American women faced. Their responsibilities were changing. More were working outside the home. Many had a hard time coping with their new way of life.

Much of Margaret's research was on the way women and men behave toward each other. Her most famous book on this subject was *Male and Female,* published in 1949. Margaret had strong views on marriage. She said that marriage was "terminable," something that could be ended when necessary. This shocked some people. Others were pleased that the subject of divorce was being discussed.

Another of Margaret's interests was the "generation gap"—when children and their parents have different ideas about things. As the years passed, she studied almost every aspect of American life. She even studied eating habits. Margaret learned so much about the way Americans live and think that the government often asked her opinion.

Margaret wrote almost thirty books, as well as hundreds of articles. She taught at several universities and was curator of the American Museum of Natural History. She had joined the museum in her early twenties, and she remained associated with it throughout her life.

By the time Margaret died, she was one of the most famous anthropologists in the world. Because of her work, social anthropology had become a major science. Equally important, she had made it understandable to ordinary people. Margaret had helped millions of people learn more about themselves and others.

Quick Notes

- Margaret had one daughter, Mary Catherine Bateson.

- In 1969, Margaret was named "Mother of the Year" by *Time* magazine.

Margaret's studies of other cultures helped her understand the problems in her own society. She specialized in studies of children and families.

"You must work very hard at the beginning. It is hard to push the door open and get inside a subject. But once you understand it, it is very interesting."

Chien-shiung Wu

American Nuclear Physicist

Early Years

Chien-shiung (Chen Shoong) grew up in China in a small town called Liuhe. There was no school for girls in Liuhe, so her father started one. It was the only girls school in the region, and it was an elementary school. It could not teach children older than nine.

Most of Chien-shiung's classmates did not go on to high school, but she wanted a full education. Chien-shiung's parents believed that girls should be as well educated as boys. They enrolled her at a boarding school in Soochow, some distance away.

Chien-shiung worked so hard at Soochow that she graduated at the top of her class. She was offered a place at the National Central University at Nanjing. There, too, Chien-shiung worked exceptionally hard. Before long, all the professors were bragging about her work.

BACKGROUNDER

Soochow Girls School

Two types of education were offered at this school: teacher training and academic studies. Chien-shiung was enrolled in the teachers course because it was free. Her family could not afford the fees for the academic course. Chien-shiung envied her friends who were doing the academic course. She persuaded them to lend her their books after they had done their homework. That was how Chien-shiung learned the sciences. Studying far into the night, she taught herself **physics**, chemistry, and math.

At the National Central University, Chien-shiung was the university's top student.

Developing Skills

After graduating with her bachelor's degree, Chien-shiung taught for a year. Then she took a research job at the National Academy of Sciences in Shanghai. Her instructor there had earned her Ph.D. degree in the United States, and she encouraged Chien-shiung to do the same.

Chien-shiung sailed for the United States in 1936. She planned to work for her Ph.D. in physics and then return home. She never saw her family again. Japan invaded China the following year, and Chien-shiung's family told her to stay in America for a while. She stayed for thirty-seven years. Not until the 1970s was it safe for her to go back to China, and then it was only for a visit.

Chien-shiung became well known as a physicist in the United States. She was an expert on fission—the splitting of the **nucleus** of an **atom**. Although the first atomic bomb had not yet been created, scientists had done much of the groundwork, including research on fission.

"I doubt that any open-minded person really believes … that women have no intellectual capacity for science and technology."

Because Chien-shiung was a woman, she was not asked to join the team of scientists that was designing the atomic bomb. Physics was still thought of as a man's subject. In some universities, women could not even study physics.

During World War II, these attitudes changed. There was a shortage of physicists, so women were hired. Chien-shiung was appointed to teach physics at Princeton University. She was the first woman to hold this position.

Chien-shiung's reputation spread. At last, in 1944, she was asked to join the team building the atomic bomb. Working at Columbia University in New York, in a former warehouse, she helped design the **radiation** detectors for the bomb.

After the war, Chien-shiung was asked to stay on at Columbia. She became an associate professor of physics in 1947 and was promoted to full professor in 1952. She was greatly respected for her high standards and hard work. Some of her students called her the Dragon Lady because she expected them to work as hard as she did.

BACKGROUNDER

The Manhattan Project

This was the name of the project to build an atomic bomb at Los Alamos, New Mexico, during World War II. The team was led by the American physicist J. Robert Oppenheimer, and included scientists from many other countries. The first successful test of the bomb occurred in New Mexico in July 1945. A few weeks later, on August 6, a bomb was dropped on the city of Hiroshima in Japan. After a second bomb was dropped, Japan surrendered and World War II ended.

Atomic bombs are some of the deadliest weapons ever invented. Several scientists who worked on the bomb later spent their lives trying to ban the bomb.

Accomplishments

I n 1956, Chien-shiung was approached by two physicists, Dr. Tsung Dao Lee and Dr. Chen Ning Yang. They had been doing research that produced odd results. It had caused them to believe that the tiny particles inside an atom might not always act according to the laws of nature.

According to one of the laws of nature, the parity principle, atoms act **symmetrically**. In other words, when the nucleus or center of an atom decays, the same number of particles will always be ejected on the right as on the left. The two researchers had begun to doubt that this was true.

Nobody had ever tried to prove this law of nature. Chien-shiung decided to try. She lined up a research team in Washington, and for the next six months she worked harder than ever. With her classes to teach at Columbia as well as her research in Washington, she had barely four hours of sleep a night.

Chien-shiung with two associates, Dr. Lee and Dr. Mo.

"*This small, modest woman was powerful enough to do what armies can never accomplish: she helped destroy a law of nature. And laws of nature, by their very definition, should be constant.*"

New York *Post*

Finally, in January 1957, her team had the answer. More particles came out one end of the nucleus than the other. This discovery led to many new developments in physics.

Drs. Lee and Yang, who had first suggested the experiments, wrote a paper about the discovery. Ten months later, they were awarded a Nobel Prize. Chien-shiung was very disappointed that she was not included in the prize.

Years before, when she was a small child in China, her father had told her, "Just put your head down and keep walking forward." Chien-shiung tried to follow his advice now. Soon, she was "walking forward" with new research projects.

By the time Chien-shiung retired in 1981, she was known as one of the world's leading physicists. Her careful experiments and dedicated work had brought her many awards and honors. These included the Wolf Prize in Physics and the National Medal of Science. In 1990, she became the first living scientist to have an asteroid named after her. It is called the Wu Chien-shiung Asteroid.

Quick Notes

- **Chien-shiung's name means "courageous hero."**

- **Chien-shiung married a fellow physicist, and they have one son.**

- **Not until 1973 was Chien-shiung able to visit China. By then, her parents and brothers were dead.**

Since retiring, Chien-shiung has traveled extensively. She gives lectures and encourages more women to become scientists.

More Women in Profile

Hundreds of women have made important contributions to science. Here are a few more. The Suggested Reading list will give you further information on these women, as well as on other women scientists.

1854–1923
Hertha Ayrton
British Inventor

Hertha first earned her living by doing needlework. In 1876, she passed the entrance exam into Cambridge University where she later taught. She was the first woman to be a member of the Institute of Electrical Engineers. Hertha's many inventions include a line divider that is still used by architects. During World War I, she also invented the Ayrton fan, used to blow away poison gas.

1858–1947
Rosa Smith Eigenmann
American Ichthyologist

Rosa's specialty was fish. She was the first American woman to become famous for her work in ichthyology, the study of fish. She was especially interested in the fish of South America and wrote many scientific papers about them.

1887–1948
Ruth Benedict
American Anthropologist

One of the most famous anthropologists in the world, Ruth was thirty-two before she began to study anthropology. Ruth believed that cultures have different characters, just as people do. Her two best-known books are *Patterns of Culture* (1934) and *The Chrysanthemum and the Sword* (1946). Ruth taught at Columbia University for many years.

Ruth Benedict

1920–1958
Rosalind Franklin
British Crystallographer and X-ray Analyst

Before she died of cancer at the age of thirty-seven, Rosalind helped make one of the most important discoveries of modern science. When working at King's College, London, in 1953, she used an X-ray camera to take pictures of **DNA**, the "building block" of living cells. At the time, no one knew what DNA looked like. Rosalind's X-rays showed that DNA was shaped in a spiral, like a corkscrew. She and her fellow researchers concluded that the structure of DNA was two interlocking spirals, called a double helix. All modern research on genes is based on this discovery.

1921–
Ursula Franklin
Canadian Physicist

An expert in the structure of metals, Ursula has applied this knowledge to archeology. By analyzing ancient tools and other objects, she has been able to say when they were made. Ursula has also gained worldwide recognition as a promoter of Science for Peace. She is very concerned about the dangers of nuclear testing. She has tried to educate people about the effect that science and technology can have on the environment.

1878–1972
Lillian Moller Gilbreth
American Industrial Engineer

Lillian was a pioneer of time-and-motion studies. These studies look at how people in offices and factories can do their work most efficiently. She developed her ideas while organizing her own family. Lillian had twelve children whom she brought up while studying for a Ph.D. in psychology. She described her ideas in *Psychology of Management* (1914) and other books. In 1948, Lillian's son Frank wrote about the family in the humorous and best-selling book *Cheaper by the Dozen.*

Lillian Moller Gilbreth

1934–

Jane Goodall

British Ethologist

Jane is virtually the founder of ethology, the study of how animals behave in the wild. In 1960, she set up camp in East Africa, in Tanzania's Gombe Stream Reserve. For more than thirty years, she studied the chimpanzees there. Her small camp has grown to become the Gombe Stream Research Centre, and Jane is known throughout the world as the leading expert on chimpanzees.

Jane Goodall

1838–1914

Margaret Knight

American Inventor

Margaret was twelve when she made her first invention. At the time, her brothers were working in a cotton mill in New Hampshire, and sometimes the **shuttles** fell from the looms and injured the workers. Margaret designed a gadget to prevent this. Most of her inventions were connected with heavy machinery. They ranged from rotary engines to shoe-making machines.

1903–1971

Kathleen Lonsdale

British X-ray Crystallographer

X-ray crystallographers study the structure of crystals. Kathleen was one of the finest crystallographers of her time. In 1945, she was elected to the Royal Society. She was one of the first two women elected to this respected group, and she later became its vice-president. In 1949, she was appointed professor of chemistry and head of the Department of Crystallography at University College, London.

1878–1968

Lise Meitner

Austrian Nuclear Physicist

Lise was the first person to realize that the **nucleus** of the **atom** can be split to release huge amounts of energy. This discovery was made in 1938. Her discovery led to the development of the atomic bomb in the 1940s. Lise refused to help make the bomb. She believed that nuclear power should be used only for peaceful purposes.

1882–1935

Amalie (Emmy) Noether

German Mathematician and Physicist

"She was by far the best woman mathematician of all time and one of the greatest mathematicians (male or female) of the twentieth century."

Jean Dieudonne, French mathematician

Emmy solved mathematical problems that helped Einstein develop his theory of relativity. In the 1920s, she paved the way for modern mathematics with her pioneering work in **algebra**.

1909–1975

Marguerite Perey

French Chemist

A brilliant chemist, Marguerite was professor of nuclear chemistry at Strasbourg University and director of the Nuclear Research Center. She was the first woman to be made a member of the Académie des Sciences.

1914–1994

Dixy Lee Ray

American Zoologist and State Governor

Dixy studied the tiny animals that attack wood under water. As director of the Pacific Science Center from 1963 to 1973, she did much to get people interested in science. She was especially concerned about the harm being done to the environment. From 1977 to 1981, Dixy was governor of Washington State.

Dixy Lee Ray

1914–1981

Barbara Ward

British Ecologist and Economist

As an **ecologist**, Barbara was very concerned about the environment. Her work as an economist made her aware of poverty in many parts of the world. From 1973 to 1980, she was president and then chairperson of the Institute for the Environment and Development. One of her best-known books is *Only One Earth: The Care and Maintenance of a Small Planet* (1972).

Glossary

algebra: a kind of math that uses letters or symbols to represent numbers

astronomy: a science that studies the sun, moon, and stars

atom: the smallest part of an element that has all the properties of the element

bulletin: a magazine or newspaper that is put out regularly

controversy: a public argument

data: information

DNA: an acid that is part of all living things

ecologist: a person who studies how living things relate to other organisms in their environment and to each other

excavate: to dig out

fungi: plantlike organisms that have no roots or leaves, such as mushrooms

malaria: a fever that is spread by mosquitoes

nucleus: the center of an atom

physics: a science that studies matter, heat, light, and sound

poacher: a person who hunts animals illegally

prehistoric: a time before recorded history

radiation: a form of energy that includes light, heat, and X-rays

radio waves: electric vibrations that carry sound

sea anemone: a brightly colored animal that lives in warm seas and has tentacles

sea urchin: a sea animal with a soft body and a spiny shell

shuttle: part of a weaving machine

species: types of plants and animals

suffragette: a woman working for votes for women

symmetrically: when both sides of an object are the same when it is divided in half

transformer: a device used for changing the voltage of an electric current

zoology: the scientific study of animals

Suggested Reading

Bailey, M.J. *American Women in Science*. Santa Barbara: Abc-Clio, 1994.

Forbes, Malcolm. *Women Who Made a Difference*. New York: Simon and Schuster, 1990.

Greene, Carol. *Rachel Carson: Friend of Nature*. New York: Children's Press, 1992.

Leakey, Mary. *Disclosing the Past*. Garden City, New York: Doubleday & Company, Inc., 1984.

McGravne, Sharon Bertsch. *Nobel Prize Women in Science*. New York: Birch Lane Press, 1993.

Mowat, Farley. *Virunga:The Passion of Dian Fossey*. Toronto: Seal Books, 1987.

Raven, Susan and Alison Weir. *Women of Achievement*. New York: Harmony Books, 1981.

Saari, Peggy. *Prominent Women of the Twentieth Century*. Detroit: UXL, 1986.

Warren, Rebecca Lowe and Mary H. Thompson. *The Scientist within You: Experiments and Biographies of Distinguished Women in Science*. Eugene, Oregon: ACI Publishing, 1994.

Yount, Lisa. *American Profiles: Contemporary Women Scientists*. New York: Facts on File, 1994.

Index

1 2 3 4 5 6 7 8 9 0 Printed in Canada 7 6 5 4 3 2 1 0 9 8